NEW

MICHIGAN VERSE

NEW

MICHIGAN VERSE

Edited by CARL EDWIN BURKLUND

With a Foreword by LOUIS UNTERMEYER

ANN ARBOR

University of Michigan Press

1940

PRINTED BY EVANS–WINTER–HEBB INC., DETROIT, MICHIGAN

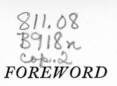
FOREWORD

Various collections of regional verse have been published to show the spread of a distinctly native culture. But this collection differs from the others in at least two ways. For one thing, it is sharply selective; scrupulously limited rather than uncritically inclusive. For another thing, it is sponsored by a great university. It is, I think, proper (if somewhat unusual) that a large educational institution should not only support scientific researches and archaeological explorations, but also encourage the creative energies of its state.

In this instance the creative energies are not inconsiderable. They are also characteristic. The reader will come upon most of the contributors with the pleasure of discovery—an adventure in a territory rich if not altogether new. There are, for example, the stern earth and ribbed quarries of Frederick ten Hoor; the vaguer, more metaphysical terrain of Theodore Roethke; the more common but quietly distinguished landscapes of Bennett Weaver and Wade Van Dore; the fertile fields of David Cornel De Jong; the traditional but not overtrodden pastures of Ivan Swift. There are, if I may dismiss the topographical metaphor, the acrid disposals in the ironic sonnets of Howard Mumford Jones; the delicate dissonances which spice the harmonies of Carl Edwin Burklund; the rich rhetoric of John Nerber; the firmly molded lyrics of Charles Miller; and the closely scrutinized experiments of John Malcolm Brinnin.

But it is not any one poet which gives this volume its quality. It is the character of the collection: the paradox of restriction and range, of particularity and variety. At first glance it may seem a somewhat arbitrary fusion; but it is a fortunate and, in its final effect, an authoritative one.

LOUIS UNTERMEYER

CONTENTS

CONTENTS

CONTENTS

CONTENTS

CONTENTS

INTRODUCTION

Anyone, I suppose, who undertakes a state anthology must feel it necessary, first of all, to explain the premise upon which it rests and the purpose he hopes it will fulfill. My premise can hardly be different from that for similar collections: the belief that it is worth doing. It is a belief that any art achievement of a state or given area has a significance no less pertinent, let us say, than its industrial achievement; that quite as important as the record of its flora or topography is the record of what it thinks and feels. Artists may not be more indispensable to a commonwealth than engineers and scientists, but neither are they less so, for the life of a people is not measured by bread alone, nor sustained by nourishment only of the mind. It is a belief that a state must regard as among its substantial records any collective art manifestation of its citizens.

My purpose has been to present such a record; to offer to the people of Michigan (and, it is hoped, to others) a representative expression of what I believe its best talent in the field of contemporary poetry. That talent, it may be urged—as Mr. Untermeyer states in his Foreword—is not inconsiderable, and, as such, is worthy of a generous response. Poets without honor at home do not, contrary to much belief, profit from such neglect; nor, in the long run, does the citizen body of whom they are a part.

Aside from what value may attach to the poetry itself, much of the interest in the present volume lies in its representative character, in the diversity in race, age, occupation, and poetic faith of the poets included. Although a glance at the biographical notes and a reading of the poems will make this apparent, I should like to note here something of this range and variety.

There is, for example, the cosmopolitan background of race, the mingling of European and native American strains. We have the German in Theodore Roethke; the Russian in Anne Persov; the Dutch in Frederick ten Hoor; the Scandinavian in E. Florence Swanson; and the American and English in Ivan Swift and A. J. M. Smith.

No less varied are the occupations of the poets. Howard Mumford Jones and Bennett Weaver are university professors; Carrow De Vries is a night watchman; David Cornel De Jong, a professional writer; Forman Brown, librettist of the Yale Puppeteers; Leona Ames Hill, a housewife; and John Nerber and Charles Miller, college students.

The difference in age among the poets presented is, roughly, bound up with differences in poetic style and treatment of material. Writers in their twenties will naturally enough be influenced by the gods of their own day. Those in their forties and fifties will speak a more familiar, because more accepted, language. In order more clearly to show this range, to allow, as it were, each generation to present itself, I have arranged the verse chronologically. From Ivan Swift, the oldest, to John Malcolm Brinnin and John Nerber, the youngest poets included, a time span is covered of about half a century. As we move from one age limit to the other, we see paralleled the general change that has taken place in the larger movement of English poetry within that period: the shift from more obvious intention and technique to the intricate and oblique persuasions of present-day writers. No collection would be adequate that did not combine the traditional patterns and the experimental tendencies of our own time.

I have stressed the representative nature of this anthology. But it must not be assumed that the poems will necessarily be Michigan poems in the sense that they convey a unique flavor. Possibly no state in our country has a life so integrated and distinct as to achieve that. Nor can it be clear to anyone what, after all, does characterize our state. We have many Michigans—the historical Michigan, rich with its legend of Indian and early explorer, of French, British, and American struggles for dominion, and of pioneer hardship; the Michigan of the spacious lumber days, of the crack of the ax and the snarl of the great saws, and of Paul Bunyan; the Michigan of meadowland and wooded hill, of crystalline lakes and cold rivers, the Michigan of vacationland. But we have also the Michigan of belts and wheels and gigantic stamping machines, of skyscrapers and expanding cities.

That relatively few of the poems in this collection are local in theme and color may to some be regrettable, but it is not necessarily a fault. Poetry has never been quite bounded by time and place. The heart is its natural home and the experience of all men its content. The special contours of that experience as determined by the rooted culture of a large area or by persuasive geographical factors (New England, let us say, or the Southwest) do not appear and may never appear. What has been intended, to repeat, is not a regional anthology in the strictest sense, but a collective record of the range that contemporary Michigan poets have expressed.

I have called the anthology *New Michigan Verse* because it is essentially new. All but six of the poets were born in the present century, and a number of them are still in their twenties. And it is new, also, in that it breaks rather sharply with the only Michigan poetry of the past of special importance—the poetry of Will Carleton. The ballads of Carleton retain, even today, a homespun dignity and a pathos effective, if at times a little obvious. But so far as I know, no quite authentic Michigan poet of the present writes in that tradition—the tradition of the 1880's. There is, further, the suggestion that to many the reading of these poets will be a new experience, for, with a few notable exceptions, they are not widely known, even among the citizens of their own state.

It may be asked: What constitutes a "Michigan" poet? I have dismissed as fruitless the search for some absolute principle of selection. Is Robert Frost, by birth a Californian, a California or a New England poet? Is T. S. Eliot more rightly American than British? It has been held as reasonable and sufficient to consider those as Michigan poets who were born and reared in the state or who, by long and established residence, have become identified with its life. Regretfully, Carl Sandburg and Edgar Lee Masters have been ruled out as unavailable, although both have lived in Michigan. They are in the public mind indelibly associated with other regions; and it would, moreover, scarcely be gracious to seek advantage on a claim so slender.

I must, finally, state a responsibility. My intention has been to make this collection as inclusive as possible, consistent with what seem to me literary standards. But after allowing for the restricted source from which I might draw, I must accept the responsibility for any fault in taste that may be apparent. The response to poetry is always personal. Nor am I confident, in spite of serious inquiry, that the volume includes all the good poets of Michigan. I can only hope that if interest should ever warrant a new edition, it will have the advantage of further information and of the collective criticism of those who may wish it well.

CARL EDWIN BURKLUND

ACKNOWLEDGMENTS

The editor makes grateful acknowledgment to the following publishers, magazines, and holders of copyright for permission to reprint poems contained in this volume.

Coward-McCann, Inc.: for selections from *Far Lake,* by Wade Van Dore. Copyright 1930, by Coward-McCann, Inc.

Henry Holt and Company, Inc.: for selections from *They Say the Forties,* by Howard Mumford Jones.

Robert Packard and Company: for selections from *Spider Kin,* by Forman Brown.

Henry Schumann: for selections from *Whatever You Reap,* by Anne Persov.

The Adelphi: for a poem by Theodore Roethke.

The Atlantic Monthly: for poems by Louisa Butler and Theodore Roethke.

The Christian Science Monitor: for poems by Leona Ames Hill.

College Verse: for poems by Elizabeth Allen and Charles Miller.

Compass: for a poem by Joseph Cherwinski.

Carrow De Vries: for a poem published originally in *The Hinterland.*

The Frontier and Midland: for a poem by Joseph Cherwinski.

Life and Letters To-Day: for a poem by John Malcolm Brinnin.

The Lyric: for poems by Carl Edwin Burklund and Joyce McIntyre.

The Midland: for poems by Frederick ten Hoor and Bennett Weaver.

The Nation: for a poem by A. J. M. Smith.

The New Republic: for poems by Theodore Roethke.

Palms: for poems by Frederick ten Hoor.

Poetry: A Magazine of Verse: for poems by John Malcolm Brinnin, Carl Edwin Burklund, David Cornel De Jong, John Nerber, Theodore Roethke, Francis Jennings Stillman, A. J. M. Smith, E. Florence Swanson, and Frederick ten Hoor.

A. J. M. Smith: for poems published originally in *The Dial* and *The Hound and Horn.*

The Southern Review: for poems by David Cornel De Jong.

Frederick ten Hoor: for a poem published originally in *Better Verse.*

Twentieth-Century Verse: for a poem by Theodore Roethke.

The Virginia Quarterly Review: for a poem by Carl Edwin Burklund.

Voices: for a poem by Frances Jennings Stillman.

The Yale Review: for a poem by Theodore Roethke.

No acknowledgments would be complete that did not express the editor's gratitude to the poets themselves and to the authorities of the University of Michigan who have made this volume possible; to a friend of the University for the funds for its publication; to Professors Arno L. Bader and Bennett Weaver for their reading of the manuscript and for helpful suggestions; and finally (and especially) to Mr. Louis Untermeyer for a continued generosity and good will.

NEW

MICHIGAN VERSE

DESCENT

It is large life to sit on the door-log
Of the Hill Tavern,
Among the distinguished birches
Standing in groups,
And look beyond the monotonous green floor
Of the matted treetops of the lower land,
To the high horizon and the barges,
And the purple island in a ring of gold.

But I am of the lowland,
Of the undistinguished trees and juniper,
And must go down the deliberate trail
Of the undistinguished dead—
And no noon.

Below the bluff-rim—
The trees now are more separate
And individual of pattern;
But the dusk marries them to one another,
And their top branches intertwine,
Like parasols in a crowded park of listeners,
As far as the path leads to the valley terrace.
Then the black belt of tamarack
And tangled bittersweet
Is like the Lower Ten, leaning on brothers
To make stand against the uncertain winds,
And dying in the smother of a brief day.

Out of this and on the far side, I knew—
And the stranger would scarce surmise
And rarely venture—
The sun dances in golden tack-points
On the near, cool shallows of the sea.
The gray islands have gone down

Over the world's rim,
And the freight barges are companion buoys
Floating in pairs under thin smoke fans.
The ring of gold is at my feet, glistening!—
Washed clean by the white surf-reefs
Broken by the blue shadow of a gull.
A single tiger lily
Flames in a whorl of beach-juniper.

IVAN SWIFT

THE BLUE CRANE

Across nine miles of calm water—
Water yet stained by the bleeding hoofs
Of the hour-gone sun—
Skillagalee Light burns like a spot-welder
Riveting a purple island to the rim of the world.
From my heavy Dutch-door pane,
When my back is to the candles and the green globe
Of my orbit-lamp, I can make out the little eye
Shining like a moored star—
Warning from my coast
All but mariners gone mad.

Two tallow dips are on my mantel,
Serving their little utmost to my fathers
Who command me to save this landmark.
How much larger is the light of Skillagalee,
Builded by engineers of the new time!
Yet the candles are at hand and of more comfort,
As the moths testify—
Though my shrine is often their burial-place.

This house, now in the making,
Is of old timber from the beaches,
Old-weather with green hangings and a navajo
And symbols of eternal things—
No longer reckoned so.
It is a quiet place full of eloquent whispers
In summer, and cedar trees perfume the lofts.
The white birch stands a trim sentry
Against the boulder patterns,
And a blue crane is at peace with the night,
On the furthermost rock along shore.

After my years of unquietness
This house is as a candle in the dark;
But it seems a burial-place of something I have known,
Or something that has been a part of me in cities,
Or something I have sensed among romping children
And the reminiscences of kinfolk
Who pass time in homely converse.

I have prepared my house to my liking,
And it lights a corner of the wilderness;
But moth-men find this a burial-place
Of a life to their liking,
And seek the larger light on the runway of the loud ships—
The light that shines like Skillagalee
Across the bleeding footprints of the sun.

At times I seem the blue crane
On the furthermost rock;
Yet the spirits of my fathers
Have aided in the laying of these stones
And the framing of these rafters,
And the Indians upon whose graves its corners are builded
Have signed these plans
And are my silent and wise company.

Let me be the man, on the rough coast,
My house of seasoned timber;
Though I seem at times like the blue crane
On the furthermost rock.
Somewhere, on other shores, in peace with night,
Are my fellows, content with little candles
In quietness, keeping the landmarks—
Content with a strong house of clean faith
And removed from the light of Skillagalee
Nine miles across the water.

IVAN SWIFT

TO A SEA-GULL

Seeing you, through the pleasant June,
Fixed on a shore-rock, like an ivory thing,
Or some, more animate, buffoon
Changing foot with foot's locality
To keep place in the noon—
Loath to move
And unconcerned to see
Even your perfect image in the pale-green cove:
One would scarce surmise
What winds were in your wing
Waiting a larger enterprise.

How will the indifference depart,
And what mad pranks
From the nursery of your brave heart
Come to the fore—
When storms bend down to sweep
The sea-floor,
And stir the dead that sleep
In the green weeds under the jetsam planks!
It is man's lamenting wonder
How that the bellowing thunder
And wild lightning and slant rain
Make you to laugh, tho' with a note of pain;
And cry mockingly, with glad laughter.
Is it that your care foretells a peace hereafter?
Or that the natural hour has come at length—
Against long waiting,
Or idle incident of mating—
With new tasks matched to your great strength?

But yesterday
One of your kinsmen lay
Quiet in my trembling hand.
Blinded by death, it was, and the wet sand.
He seemed not less than your own image,
In the shore-surf; and not once ill at ease
Had this white body been, nor worse for damage
Nor perturbed by struggle with calamities.

Thou, bird of more than grace and beauty—
Sleek house-ward of the rooms of bight and bay;
Friend of man and sexton in thy casual duty—
Take me to brotherhood this day!
My morning and the warm sun have stood me long,
And I am weary of the rest
And the old monotony of mating-song;
And I am tired of my own nest
And my own image in the still pools of the west.
Teach me thy fearlessness of thunder
And the wind, and the red rain that is—
Over the nations! Failing this—
Teach me, O bird-god, faith and calm wonder!

IVAN SWIFT

LANDING

These trees and plants—birch, hemlock and pine,
Dogwood and bittersweet—
Are of the soil that is my soil.
This breeze is our breath,
This lake and fog and sun our common nourishment.
We take on life here—leaf and flower;
Become of use and comfort to the wild-life,
And, next to wild-life, the childlike Indian
Fixed in his place and pride.
And he, without aspiration or complaint,
Keeps us in turn patient, by example,
To grow, gradual as the oak, in fiber, limb and symmetry,
Beyond the cutting and consuming world;
And stays our youth of dreams and legendary visions.

Let those who will, burn the paved hills
And web the sky on iron wings;
They describe circles, large or small,
And shall make landing here—
Where we cultivate in peace and wait in silent praise.

IVAN SWIFT

THE ECHO TO THE SEA

Your law shall take a star along
    An upward orbit twined with space;
But what shall be the law of song,
    And laughter in the human face?

Though there the unseen ether lifts
    The swelling deep and Betelguese,
What force can stay the mind that drifts
    To something vaster far than these?

Drifts and is wrecked—oh, what can stay
    The heart, or swing it into poise?
It shakes among the powers of day
    And in the night it hears a noise

Of chaos rushing to the spill.
    Where shall it find a central doom?
Where shall it know that ease of will
    Which tides know, moving under spume?

The cave gives echoes to the sea,
    The cliff gives back the bounding cry,—
The trouble of infinity
    Is yet to cherish what would die!

Let man whose mind is split in twain
    Trust yet the secret, if he can,
Nor guess too soon that all is vain,
    Nor be too sure that man is man.

BENNETT WEAVER

OUT OF THE EARTH

The earth is deeper than we guess
   And full of things we shall not know;
We are but arrow leaf and cress
   Withered against the brook's thin flow.

We are the thorn tree on the knoll
   Rising enough to stand and cut
The wind, and cry and give her soul
   Out to the dark. Our veins are shut.

We are chink-lichen fastened tight
   Against the boulder which the plow
Must turn out from. And in the night
   The dark frost breaks the roots—as now!

We are the drift of a hot cloud
   Over the flame-land of the west,
And while the fields are singing loud
   We veer and turn to ashen rest.

Ours is a house whose doors are barred,
   Whose oilless lamps no hand can move:
The lintels there are scratched and scarred
   By the fierce returning thoughts of love.

BENNETT WEAVER

THROUGH WINDOWS

Through windows that some dream has raised
   We reach our hands into the night;
We feel the breath of hovering things
   And touch their pale, sweet light.

We hold in shadows softly dim
   Those forms which never hands may hold,
And press the throbbing brows of those
   Whom death made mute and cold.

It were at last a little thing
   To lean too far across the sill,
To sense some beckoning touch and go
   When all the winds are still.

BENNETT WEAVER

LOST

The creep of the gold sea
  Up the silver of the sand,
A white sail cutting the white moon,
  A cry from land.

A long path over the moor,
  A pale path away from the foam:
One soul to the moon on the waters,
  And one, home.

BENNETT WEAVER

TENNYSON'S FATHER

He lies beneath a bitten cross,
   Beneath a gnarled grave-poisoned yew;
And old winds wrangle in the moss
   For cups of stale and sour dew.

Over his tomb the weary sun
   Drops a pale slant of senile flame;
And who is he? The moss alone
   Holds in her little roots his name.

BENNETT WEAVER

THE FORTIES

There'll be dancing in the clubs when we are done for,
There'll be cocktail drinking still at all the bars,
And other girls will call for men in cars,
And other lovers ask what they'd begun for
And wonder what God made the earth and sun for,
And other wives create domestic jars
When other husbands under other stars
Repudiate the prizes they had run for.

But Hemingway has taught us we were tragic,
And Faulkner has informed us we were queer,
And Mr. Eliot with destructive magic
Decoyed us to the Wasteland, and we're here;—
Is it so strange we feel our isolation,
Hung midway between madness and damnation?

HOWARD MUMFORD JONES

THE FORTIES

The young men ask me questions, the young girls shyly
Propound me questions, knowing that I must know.
Have I not loved a thousand years or so?
I answer their inquiries a little dryly,
And if you watch, you will see me smiling wryly
As I dispose of God or sex in a flow
Of aphorism; and when we have talked, they go,
Bewildered a little, but still regarding me highly.

And shall I answer them sagely out of Carlyle?
Shall I tell them that life is labor, defeat a duty?
Shall I tell them the end is laughter, and speak of grace?
Shall I tell them all that remains at the last is beauty,
When the arteries harden, a picture, a phrase, a face?
Shall I tell them the bitter truth? Would it be worth while?

HOWARD MUMFORD JONES

THE FORTIES

Mrs. Maria Zloty, mother of four
(There is a wood in Poland, a wood and a river,
And I think the dark stream will flow through my heart forever),
Mrs. Maria Zloty stood in the door
Waiting, while the company ambulance bore
(I gave my heart to the hawks, my gift to the giver—
Will it be today, my lover, tomorrow or never?)
The body of Zloty home, to come home no more.

The communist stood on the Zloty porch
(And the moon goes down in the dark on a dim, dark head),
And the widow Zloty, staring from two immense
Sarmatian eyes, offered him twenty-five cents
(My love was a beautiful lover, my lover is dead)
To subscribe to *The* (published in English) *Workers' Torch*.

HOWARD MUMFORD JONES

THE FORTIES

The communist orators talk on and on;
They fill the squares, the street-corners, the parks;
They preach the gospel according to St. Marx
With the fire of Christian martyrs; their phrases run
Like liturgies that never will be done;
They are holy men divinely scattering sparks,
Humorless Noahs building communal arks
To save us when the flooding waters run.

God moves in a mysterious way and odd
His wonders to perform. His patience is great.
He made the snake, the tapeworm, and the bear;
He made the mosquito and the millionaire;
Torture and beauty are His, and so is fate.
Shall we be more intolerant than God?

HOWARD MUMFORD JONES

THE FORTIES

Item: we bequeath to you speed; also the clean
Whirring of dynamos; the float and dive
Of planes; gangsters; muck; the charity drive;
Ballyhoo; graft; every superb machine;
Death in the midnight alleyways; the lean
Strength of the swiftest runners now alive;
Roads like a curving arrow; shacks where hive
Intemperance and filth; the latest movie queen.

Item: we also leave you certain hours
When tenderness comes, and green are the ancient trees;
Sunset; and dreaming meadows where spring has birth;
Shy birds on dew-drenched bushes; faint young flowers;
Love also, and death, and birth. We will you these,
Knowing, my children, you shall inherit the earth.

HOWARD MUMFORD JONES

BURNING BRUSH

Blue smoke and a bright flame
    entangle among dry brittle
    brush piled for a ready burning,
    but this net cannot hold fire
    and is rent and becomes dust.

He watches the quick flames darkly,
    knowing he had a man's right
    to make earth bear something
    beside scrub oak—but had he?

The tops of young trees that had grown
    intimately in sunlight, hidden
    shy quavers of song, that had borne
    sleet with a curving declension
    and snow delicately, now
    crackle and hiss and become ash.

A singeing spark of regret
    from the bright burning now falls
    into the troubled mind, lord of so much
    that is not of its own contriving.

FREDERICK TEN HOOR

THE CATERPILLAR LEAF

A caterpillar ripples across my path—
A hairy motion into and out of sunlight
Indefinitely patterned by moulting trees—
And vanishes among the colored leaves.
The one I lift to find him is ochreous,
Imperfect, beetle-bitten, slug-defiled,
Stained by disaster, and then incredibly
Beautiful in my hand, as if it were
The portrait of itself by one who knew
The last requirement of foliage.
It is a thing to treasure, but not to keep;
Better to let it fall, flutter slowly
To settle upon its fellows dusted by death,
And offer me the memory of this perfection:
A leaf in the mind, like a caterpillar
Upon its way to spin a dark cocoon,
Later to emerge and mean something
Unpredictable by a man strolling
No matter how thoughtfully among dead leaves.

FREDERICK TEN HOOR

DO NOT PITY THE DEAD

Do not pity the dead that they have gone
Leaving unfinished what they did not begin;
Out of nothing they came, the cut stone
Marks the return—there is no sound within.

They loved and suffered and made little or much
Out of breath of air and earth's plenitude.
If aught was theirs, it was to see and touch;
Each had his chance, why should it be renewed?

Or why should it last, did they live so well?
Did any man live as if he understood?
Do not pity the dead; for no one can tell
Whether their going was ill or subtly good.

FREDERICK TEN HOOR

AGAINST THIS SILENCE

The trees we walked among were very still
And dark against the gleaming of a hill
Blue-white with snow, made colder by the light
From something very far and very bright.

Seeing this immobility that willed
So resolutely nothing, we were stilled.
Against this silence, what was there to say
By creatures that live shrilly for a day?

FREDERICK TEN HOOR

THE GREBE

Aimless and cold
   Velocities,
Snow points make lines
   Among the trees;

Black water stirred
   By a flaked wind
Chips under willows
   Starkly thinned;

An oval float,
   Perhaps a bird,
Allows a croaking
   To be heard—

No song, no call,
   But merely sound,
A crack in silence
   Winter-bound.

FREDERICK TEN HOOR

SINGING RAIN

Who attends
The fall of rain
Not on garden
Nor on grain.

Not for profit
Nor for loss,
But on thistle
And on moss,

He shall see
With dear surprise
Beauty hid
From other eyes;

He shall feel
Within him growing
All the knowledge
Worth the knowing.

He shall never
Lack again
Living water,
Singing rain.

FREDERICK TEN HOOR

EASTER BY A RIVER

Here is a quarry long forgotten;
The shaft is plugged, its timbers rotten
And green with moss again like trees
Refurbished since their calvaries.

And here a river gutters through
A town no Christ is coming to;
No living stream, these waters lave
A populous and noisy grave.

O Easter bells in towers blunted,
The man is gone your clergy hunted!
The tomb is closed again. Come, see
A toad and other pleasantry.

Only the grass beside this well
Is cousin to a miracle;
And also moss upon a tree
Approximately comforts me.

FREDERICK TEN HOOR

ECLIPSE

Christ walks upon the water tonight
Alone, with no one on his right

And no one on his left; alone
As cold as death, as hard as stone.

He walks away from the tossing boat
Where a fisherman casts the deciding vote;

He walks away from the dock, where Mary
Waits for the raucous Jersey ferry;

Out to sea, where the night is dark,
Toward the Leviathan and the Shark.

Pray if you must on bended knees;
Christ is as deaf as the least of these.

He will not hear, he will not turn;
His heart is dry in a Christian urn.

Christ walks out toward sea tonight,
His white hands clenched, his lips shut tight.

FREDERICK TEN HOOR

SONG FOR COMFORT

I am hurt. I am dismayed.
And my thirst is unallayed;
There is nothing more to see
Of a dreamed felicity.

Still my heart is well content
To have been so violent;
And the twisted mouth will sing
About almost anything.

For the rapture I have known
Was not carven on a stone;
And the honey and the bread
Was not ever merited.

Wherefore, then, should I demur?
Beauty is my comforter.
And my bright and sovereign lord,
Shall design the final word.

FREDERICK TEN HOOR

EUMENIDES

It was not solitude alone that slew him,
The dull precision of the days that passed.
He smiled at time that trusted to undo him,
But more than time remembered him at last.

Elusive fingers leafing quiet books,
The poised resistance of a tranquil chair,
Expectancy that held the garden nooks,
And one that walked in silence with him there.

Voices that spoke with unevasive candor
Through the long syllables of evening rain,
And nights that stabbed with now familiar slander,
And doors that opened and that closed again.

These, and the slow grimaces of a curtain,
Or pictures tilted in facetious winking—
These were enough to make a man uncertain,
And set far colder eyes than his to blinking.

And in the end they had their way and slew him—
It was not solitude and not regret—
Too many things there were that would pursue him,
That would not pardon and would not forget.

CARL EDWIN BURKLUND

SONG FOR MONA

Loosen the fillet, go where water silvers
The green air;
Throw to the icy heart of a leafed pool
Your dark hair.

Smite it with music, scourge it with softness,
Cleave it with proud
Line after stinging line of darkness—shower
A cloud

Of insolent beauty. Why should it knowing
All that is known
Forever of bird-breast, star, and tapering leaf
Forever be stone?

Giving for so much given only the cool
Impertinent stare
Of silver. Loosen the fillet, go to the pool
With your shadowy hair.

CARL EDWIN BURKLUND

PAUSE AT THE YEAR'S END

Seeing the separate years, how they diminish
our once abandon; how the definite sun
measures retreating arcs. Seeing the relish
of touch, sound, color, fatefully withdrawn.

Seeing the high, the incontestable fact
crumble at length; the faltering abridgment
of that sworn treasury of love whose act
lessens the word when summoned to the judgment—

With what, I say, shall then my hour of pride
be furnished? What equivocal fulfillment
waits at the end whereto the year has died
in wisdom gathered of the heart's annulment?

CARL EDWIN BURKLUND

I HAD FORGOTTEN

I had forgotten how the water tarried,
Moving meadow-ward with its soft and silver burden;
And how the wind from a dark thicket carried,
Heavy and cool, the scent of a wildwood garden.

I had forgotten how the silence followed—
The cornfields lost, the drowsy blur of a bell—
When the great moon rolled heavenward out of a poplar;
I had forgotten the night could be so still.

CARL EDWIN BURKLUND

LOST

Listen again.
What do you hear?
Trees.
Trees touching the wind with their topmost leaves.
What do you see?
Leaves. Leaves mounting away to the tops of trees;
Darkness engulfing the deep wet moss;
The sunken track of a moose . . . .
Then we must sleep.
Yes, we must find a place to sleep,
And ask that the wandering dark be kind,
And the pointed stars,
And the heavy wind,
To you, my body,
And me, my mind.

WADE VAN DORE

THERE MUST BE SOMETHING HIGH

There must be something high
More than the stars and sky.
Something more than any light
Shining in the day or night,
That pulls at things below.
Little does the earth let go.
No matter how it tries,
The body cannot rise.
No bird can get away.
The butterfly must stay.
The flower bends at last.
These things the earth holds fast.
But they are heavy things.
A song has able wings.
When it begins to flow,
The earth will let it go.

WADE VAN DORE

DOWN TO LAKES

Down to lakes go trails that feet
Have worn upon the fragrant ground.
They come from valleys filled with heat;
They come from hills that trees have crowned.

For lakes are clearings in the land,
That ever draw down men to think,
And ever draw deer down that stand
And look awhile before they drink.

So to each lake a trailway winds,
That men may think, and grip it slow—
The thing unfolding in their minds;
That deer may flee the thing they know.

WADE VAN DORE

PADDLING

Something seems to hold the breeze
From waving water into bars—
Black water rimmed with silent trees
Holding groups of silent stars.

Something seems to wait for sound.
My paddle spills a few dark drops,
But when the moon comes rising, round,
Even that faint trickling stops.

My gaze is subject to this sight
Above the forest, rising, pale,
Gilding grey the dark of night,
Starting loons to fish and wail.

Beyond an interval of hills,
A lone moose calls; and waits.
How faint the echo fills and fills
The air, before it dissipates.

I drift until I hear again
The far-away and lonely call
Burdening the night with pain,
Drifting, dying over all.

The night has opened all its doors.
The waves I make, like silver bars,
Swim gently off toward the shores
And multiply the golden stars.

WADE VAN DORE

THE REFLECTION

No airy wind had touched the sunken lake,
And it had grown so still it barely showed
Beneath the crowded trees about its edge.
Reflected to its smallest leaf or cone
Each pointed tree went deeply, darkly in.
The vague blue sky went deeper, further down.
A deer beside it might have seen a cloud
By merely looking downward past its feet.
Still as the lake, I sat reflecting too.
But when the evening came my mind's dream ended.
So I descended to the darker lake
To touch and break its water with my hand,—
And lo, the sky began to run and shake;
The liquid forest surged as if in wind,
And broke in many fragments, soundlessly.

WADE VAN DORE

AN OLD MAN STARES AT THE MOON

An old man walks by the sea,
a shaking cane in his hand.
He looks at the moon; his feet
shuffle the sand.

His face is the crumpled page
of an ancient prayer; his lips
are brown as the windless sails
of fishing ships.

They open and close again.
There is no word, no tune.
He only shivers and stares
into the moon.

What must I do, old man,
that when I too am old
I may not find like you
the moonlight cold,

I may not stare like you
and find the moonlight chill?
He creeps on marble-eyed
and shivers still.

FORMAN BROWN

SEA NIGHT

I had forgot the sea at night
up from the black
ruffled and frothed to lacy white
in the ship's track.

I had forgot a star could make
across the sea
straightly and pallidly a track
from it to me.

I had forgot the light of the mast
above like a star
yellow through sweeping mist—
now free, now far.

I had forgot the sting of the air,
feel of the salt
sea-wind's harsh and silken snare
I once felt.

The sweetening sense of sea at night,
of night at sea
comes like a sea-gull's swerving flight
to memory;

comes like a gull to a ship where men
once gave it bread,
with little curving cries through the spin
of joy and dread.

FORMAN BROWN

TRANSFIGURATION

Cold blue the night,
cold blue the moon,
my breath was white
as moth cocoon:
a night so chill
my careful tread
creaked—and was still,
creaked—and was dead.
Then—window glow:
through festooned frost
above, below,
half seen, half lost
in forest lake,
in lake and fern,
in fern and brake
a tendril's turn
revealed your hand
and then your face
in fairyland
of frozen lace.

FORMAN BROWN

THE DEAD SAILOR

Now is he home from his long faring,
  Borne in on a tide
Over which no winds were blowing
  And no gull cried.

For him salt on the lip no longer,
  Wind and foamy wave.
Instead an elm's roots and lichen
  For a grave.

But sometimes when the blue star-glitter
  Hangs above and around,
And wind soughing in the long grasses
  Makes a sea-sound,

He will hear thunder of water
  Pounding through the gloom,
And silently will arise and go forth from
  His narrow room,

To meet the dimly flowing horizon
  Of a sea strange and stark,
Where a white sail flaps and bellies
  Against the dark—

A ghostly sail that he will follow
  Out into the night,
Tide-borne toward a new haven
  And a far light.

MYRTLE ADAMS

SHADOWS THERE ARE

Shadows there are, but shadows such as these
Are shadows only in the mortal mind,
Blown by the spirit, or the spirit's wind.

Yet shadows I have seen, of me deemed deeper,
That backed on nothing in the horrid air,

And try as try, I cannot limn the form
That some of them assume where I shall pass.
They grow transparent, and as sharp, as glass.

A. J. M. SMITH

PROTHALAMIUM

Here in this narrow room there is no light;
The dead tree sings against the window-pane;
Sand shifts a little, easily; the wall
Responds a little, inchmeal, slowly, down.

My sister, whom my dust shall marry, sleeps
Alone, yet knows what bitter root it is
That stirs within her; see, it splits the heart—
Warm hands grown cold, grown nerveless, as a fin,
And lips enamelled to a hardness—
Consummation ushered in
By wind in sundry corners.

This holy sacrament was solemnized
In harsh poetics a good while ago—
At Malfy and the Danish battlements,
And by that preacher from a cloud in Paul's.

No matter: each must read the truth himself,
Or, reading it, reads nothing to the point.
Now these are me, whose thought is mine, and hers,
Who are alone here in this narrow room—
Tree fumbling pane, bell tolling,
Ceiling dripping and the plaster falling,
And Death, the voluptuous, calling.

A. J. M. SMITH

LIKE AN OLD PROUD KING IN A PARABLE

A bitter king in anger to be gone
From fawning courtier and doting queen
Flung hollow sceptre and gilt crown away,
And breaking bound of all his counties green
He made a meadow in the northern stone
And breathed a palace of inviolable air
To cage a heart that carolled like a swan,
And slept alone, immaculate and gay,
With only his pride for a paramour.

O who is that bitter king? It is not I.

Let me, I beseech thee, Father, die
From this fat royal life, and lie
As naked as a bridegroom by his bride,
And let that girl be the cold goddess Pride.

And I will sing to the barren rock
Your difficult, lonely music, heart,
Like an old proud king in a parable.

A. J. M. SMITH

GOOD FRIDAY

This day upon the bitter tree
Died One who had He willed
Could have dried up the wide sea
    And the wind stilled.

It was about the ninth hour
He surrenderèd the ghost,
And His face was a faded flower
    Drooping and lost.

Who then was not afraid?
Targeted, heart and eye,
Struck, as with darts, by godhead
    In human agony.

For Him, who with a cry
Could shatter if He willed
The sea and earth and sky
    And them re-build,

Who chose amid the tumult
Of the darkening sky
A chivalry more difficult—
    As Man to die,

What answering meed of love
Can finite flesh return
That is not all unworthy of
    The God I mourn?

A. J. M. SMITH

THE GIFT

I shall carry a basket woven of grasses,
Pale green, and sweet with the good smell
Of summer; I shall go where the wind passes
Softly, in weather clear as a rung bell.

I shall carry a basket filled with apples,
Apples as yellow as buttercups, apples brown
As rusty leaves, and wax-red ones. The dapples
Of light through sunny trees shall filter down,

And the paths of fall be flecked with the gold color
Of sun on bright leaves. I shall come to you
With a basket of apples to keep till days be duller
And the gold be gone and the gifts of earth be few.

LEONA AMES HILL

LULLABY IN AUTUMN

What lullaby can I make you now, with the autumn
Come again to this land, come to my door,
With blue, smoke-bitter wind flinging a handful
Of yellow-bright beech leaves across the floor?

How can I sing you to sleep with the mists lying
Whiter than wool across the river plain,
And the maple trees shouting and wearing their scarlet
And russet-hued robes in the windy rain?

How can you sleep at all? There are apples glowing
Crimson and amber, rich on the orchard boughs,
And you and I shall run to the orchard tomorrow
And bring wind-fallen apples to the house.

LEONA AMES HILL

PRAYER ON A NEW YEAR'S EVE

Crooked fingers, you have again bent
And knuckled-out, scratched and thumped away,
Pointed into or cramped upon another year.
Write at this hour of strident bells that pent
And hazardous clause that is to be the epitaph—
Your sagging bushel full of months and years—
Where this road of gravel ends upon your own
Most cold and horizontal flesh at last
Stripped clean of every detriment.

Roar bells, then sink upon the wind-drained sound
Away to the unknown hell from which this year came
That marches into my veins. Fill, great gong
Of the sky, the flat street beneath where pound
A legion of voices upon an answerless void.
To yesterday's fences we tethered the goats
With our sins, the sheep with our pardons, but
They bleat on and tomorrow we only have time
To feed what is pleasant and round.

Lay on your lap your conscience' face,
Fingers, stroke the eyes, the soft cheek. And weep
For the dreams you meant to have loved again
And nourished and clad, those small of grace
Lost under the wheels. The least of your little ones,
Father: forgive that our cups were few,
And the wheel of days too fast for any stay,
Or mercy unto all the things we begot
But gave no strength for time or space.

DAVID CORNEL DE JONG

LAND OF MILK AND HONEY

Here the broad shepherd comes—lambs bruising
The purple clover in his wake. On the boulder
Birds turn, and their grave eyes see his pulse
Throbbing against the sea of June, his lips choosing
The rosy words that mean feast and banquet
For the furrows, for all the hefty bulls.

Shower him black-and-white singers—spread whither
He treads all the round songs. Here is laurel,
Tormentil and rose to circle his brow, to lie
There and be lovely. Let careful lizards slither;
He has a stride of peace, a throat ready
For the organ-madrigal that speeds him by.

So sleep populous hill; stoop bough, deeply
To let him eat fruit honeyed and yellow
Wherever he reaches. Some man, little in bone
And strength shall see him there, and cheaply
His afterthoughts shall run to raveled-out legends
Wherein God carried sheep, but hungered alone.

Cool dew, cold rain, chilly lake and river,
Winter of the lonely crying, he is here wearing
His love. Swift cloud, kneel at last on the hill,
This is our peaceful companion, the giver
Of boon; now all the moor hens and foxes scud proudly
To every golden sun, and evil has no will.

My knotted generation, stoned eyes, see proudly
This is the way he walked, that path swaying
With light. We are alone with seasons we forgot,
Clutch close the big thing remembered, speak loudly
On the slopes. We, who saw all tenderness bleeding,
Must harbor briefly this mid-day dream we trusted not.

DAVID CORNEL DE JONG

SOLILOQUY DURING SORROW

Consider, after all those days of heavy falling,
that we remembered not at all, not once
the lofty things, the mocking birds rippling
the evening out in carols, and all the wrens;
but found again the sorrows of soughed out months,
and knew only the sycamore's nightward sighing.
Then all the thoughts on all the dead swelled higher,
as if the dead themselves were tides from an old shore
with its bliss depleted, where children shouted never.

Sometimes deep seasons must come like this, with
no one to palliate the valley's ruthless going
to yellow, the teeth then stand upon the lips,
and in the mind the swans keep swinging toward
sandy tomorrows. Some mouth in a sunny courtyard
may say it is only yesterday's defeats whereof
the grapes are sour, but tomorrow's plums hang full.
Still, our eyes peer out of the tightened windows
and our garden gate is bolted and we speak with
the gaunt angels hoarsely in our blackened houses.

Surely, in due time we shall no longer sit,
twining our fingers like limp reeds together,
as if our thoughts were braiding themselves stronger
baskets to hold all the season's falls and plunders;
and our hands shall lie still upon our thighs once more,
when we shall hear the clarions tremble over the waters
where our wonders first floundered. Perhaps we shall
rise at the first piquant bleating of lambs and go,
tall and more mellowed, along the paths again
to husband our flocks and speak most tenderly
to these our heavy beasts we guide and follow.

Yes, but today we must hold the dead a little while
longer, see them among April's tumults, hear their
jocund songs lilting, and feel their fingers as on
the delicate pears, with all fruits velveting for
their tasting. Recall—remember, unto the utmost
source of recalling, until the dead are so very loud,
that we lie like fallow fields beneath their shouting—
beneath their black-crow calling—until even remembering
has seeped into the earth, and at last grass spears out,
beetles unfurl, and the earliest bee tumbles with our thoughts
onto the diapason hum of the living, and we see our slow
bodies follow to spread the hands for sun and sowing.

DAVID CORNEL DE JONG

QUESTION

Once we had fields for our hopes, the lakes
Along our plantings full of morning glowing.
What is it that months do, that time takes,
To find now only a slope in day snowing
Its old colds, where once we harrowed so well,
Where we spoke, heads to the soil, hearing
The gulls above, as if hearing could quell
Their white petulance on all our fearing?

What have the years done when never we saw
The seeping away of dreams amid our toiling,
Never the ending, till at last the air was raw
With crows, with grackles, and harvest spoiling
Upon the stalks, when we bent no more and fear
With youth had gone like wren and swallow
Beyond all sight, and crows came very near
To scratch the earth already still and fallow?

The days have dropped unto snow, the sky
At last lies close against all wonder
That nothing may breathe, nothing ask why
It was the gulls we dared not hear, not thunder
Or bellowing beasts on a neighboring hill,
Only the white birds high, and their silver falling
Never for the eyes, only for ears, so long until
Even earth was stilled of fear and naked calling.

DAVID CORNEL DE JONG

SIMPLE LEGEND

We built us a house, while
the compassionate hills lay around
and the sun made shadows for our
going out and blessed our coming in.

But nearby we found bones in the grass,
a bird ascended and threw down
note upon scolding note, and then
that day, too, ended at last.

Sometimes the hills crawled nearer
and said things we ought to have heard
in words, but we made of it music
with no consequence or hurt.

And with no literate faith we
gave the wolves of our bread;
if winter comes, we thought, we
shall be untouchable and bold.

Nothing came, no winter came, even
swans rode upon our lake, but
very soon the walls we had built
were inanimate no more;

they talked with the hills, they lay
in their arms at night, dew
hallowed everything, but we, left
small and alone, grew a little afraid.

It was before snow came, when we
peering outside heard the swans
selling our flesh and saw the hills
grin at remembering our tenderness.

On a hoarse November while stripped
earth cowered around we ran,
leaving behind three old minds which
sometimes come whispering at night.

Then we run again, pursued by hill
and swan and wolf, understanding
at last we should not have found bones
but dandelions in the grass.

DAVID CORNEL DE JONG

DESERTED CHURCH

In this distant place among the hills,
I came upon a long deserted church.
The dream of some self-styled son of god
To save the souls of his people
In this quiet valley.
Perhaps he had died, or his dream had.
How was I, a stranger, to know?

CARROW DE VRIES

WAYNE COUNTY

I miss my native hills.
I like not these wide stretches of flatland.
I want Paul Bunyan to come back.
I will take him to Trenton
And entertain him with a hundred barrels of Trenton Valley.
Then I will say, Come, Paul, you have work to do.
I will take him to the middle of Wayne County
And say, Paul, smack your giant hand down hard on the earth.
He will slam his open hand down hard.
The earth will shoot up through his fingers
And land with a thud as hills.
I will have my hills.
Paul will have a big drunk.
Next day he will have a huge headache.

CARROW DE VRIES

GIVE ME A DIME

A laborer for the moment destitute
Approaches me on the street saying,
Give me a dime, I ain't worked lately.
I say, You see I have good clothes.
I have money. I am well-fed.
Your begging embarrasses me
As well as you. I am also
Not poor enough to give you alms.
On his face I see the fear
I have seen on the faces
Of the sane in the presence of the insane
As he turns and hurries away.

CARROW DE VRIES

IF THE LILIES ARE DOWN

If the lilies are down, if the tall lilies are gone,
And no sweet yellow apples lie on the lawn,
Yet in the deep green gloom of the chestnut tree
A vireo, low and meditatively,
Sings to himself, and to a wondering Me.

Always in my mind a child lingers
At the window by the dense green leaves, and fingers
A book, wondering whether the melody
Of a human voice or a vireo would be
Sweetest to have . . . a child wonders in me.

I have forgotten to answer the hundred things
The child is asking . . . or is it the bird, that sings
Immortal in its bower in the deep shade,
Fixed in a summer that can never fade,
Where all sunlight gathers, all dews are made?

Whoever questions, child or bird, shall hear
Only an echo, repeated small and clear.
I have only come to question again
What songs are sweetest, the songs of birds or men;
Yet echo changes the question spoken then.

Unanswered questions, questions outliving time,
Grow dear as an old companion, sweet as a rhyme.
Questions we murmur to eternity
Lift us from dust: a timeless self I see
Brooding in the deep shadow of the tree.

Child, I have heard men sing, and they sang well.
They spoke of rapture, melancholy, farewell;
And still their songs had not the innocence
Of a bird's warbling, that enchants the sense
With a limpid coolness untroubled by pretense.

Yet all our listening is with human ears.
It may be bird-song, cool against our fears,
Airily ringing outside our warmest joys,
Will always, for men, be too remote a voice
To tempt any but the weary to its choice.

If the lake is quiet and the stars are veiled,
And sleep has soothed the little owl that wailed,
I will yet know: outside is the chestnut tree
Where the bird sang, sweet and unceasingly,
To the sheltering leaves, and to the child in me.

LOUISA BUTLER

GRIFFINS' WOODS

All day the leaves are drifting, slanting, fluttering,
Falling like apples on the crimson ground,
Turning like butterflies, twisting and veering,
Falling suddenly with a crisp dry sound;
Falling in sunlight, while their scarlet surfaces
Are printed on blue sky, turning their pale
Silvery undersides, catching at branches,
Swirling in gusts of wind, pelting like hail.
Then back to quiet, sifting through the sunlight,
Falling lightly, freed without a sound;
All day the foliage moves from golden branches
To lay itself upon the golden ground.
Rose-red, clear orange, garnet, olive, russet,
All day the leaves move past, come down and down,
Until the colors, like a bright mosaic,
Glow in the sun—prelude to winter brown.
And ever but one thing fills the slow hours,
One movement fills the air, one sound is heard,
The scampering sound of leaves running in companies,—
Unless the tiny *chink* of some small bird
Wanders among the yellow bushes, following
A pathway of its own, and dies away,
While still the leaves fall, in a sunny silence,
A colored silence, falling all the day.
Until the silver moon, hard-edged and definite,
Looks through bare boughs as clear and cold as she,
And shines upon the store of winter covering
Prudently massed beneath the silvered tree.
And still the leaves above whisper, "Tomorrow
Will be another day of drifting down,
Downward, downward, feeling the pull of earth,

Until in her vast sea of leaves we drown."
Now autumn in a million lovely fragments
Is falling from the trees, is drifting slowly
Through ceremonial hush, in sunny waiting,
Till on the earth she lies, divorced and lowly.
Her requiem, the twitters of small birds;
Her epitaph, a sadness in the air,
Where aromatic odors, damp and pungent,
Pervade the woods and linger, like a prayer.

LOUISA BUTLER

CITY SUNSET

The only quiet, the isolated serenity,
All of the stillness and softness, is in the sky
And the transfiguring mist, and the static mist-veiled red
Of the lights, in a long vista enclosing movement.
At the ends of streets and behind green hospital grounds,
Above the blocks of stores and the factory chimneys,
Is the magnetic tenderness of sunset cloud,
The dreamy rose and the high clear delicate blue.
In the west a crescent moon hangs over the market.
The homeward automobiles, the huge unwieldy trucks
Turned, with consummate skill, on invisible lines,
The people waiting patiently for the moment
To dart across, the cement workers laying down canvas
Over their unfinished work, the children shouting to each other—
They are conscious, perhaps of a serene remoteness,
A rose and purple reflected in streetcar windows,
A dream world superimposed, or lost, or remembered,
A something to be found instead of worked for and fought for,
A firm unshakable reward in the fight for something else,
An irrelevant glory, changeless, generous and comforting.

LOUISA BUTLER

COCK-CROW

Again down nebulous, fictive fields
Cocks crow in multitude and the night's
    procession of many lanterns wearies.
—Daybreak is yet far off.

Rain comes to mind, a half-snow beating
    invisibly into the world.
Across the wet deserted yards
A night-light wastes and splutters on a wall . . . .

Dread stirs about the room with insignificant
    gesture,
Touching a hollow wall, a still chair . . . .

IVAN OLSON

IDYL

Nothing to do here but to lie
gazing,
blue of eye
as the cold water, the far sky.

Nothing to ponder,
lying hand in hand,
but hair, golden
as the sun, as the shifting sand.

IVAN OLSON

PITY THE DEAD

Pity the dead, who lie in impervious prisons,
With their still hands precisely folded, and their eyes
Forever bandaged against the surprise of morning.

Lest they should ever come forth in happier disguise;
Lest they should ever become as free as wind and rain,
They are constrained to lie as dead men ever.

Now while I live there have been walls enough
To keep me from the full sweet savor of living,
And when I die I would have even my flesh release me.

E. FLORENCE SWANSON

HUNTER'S WIFE

Here the ordered kitchen glows
With clean daylight as you pluck
From the fragrance of its flesh
One by one the rabbit's bones.

Here the paper-thin frail shape
Of pelvic wings, and the alert
Curve of backbone, and each rib,
Delicate as spoken frost.

Do not think that these at all
Ever knew the crisped grass,
Shaken silver in the moon,
Or the secret paths of fern;

Ever crouched with stiffened breath,
Or loped like shadow through the night;
Nor imagine the bright eye
Glazing with its garnet blood;

Wrap the inarticulate bones,
And close your mind to all of this,
Lest fed like Midas, of the best,
Ashes lie upon your tongue.

E. FLORENCE SWANSON

ELEGY

When spring-time comes, think not the hearts
That war has mingled in this sod,
Find any peace who died in hate,
Though earth should put soft colors on.

Beneath the grass no roots are green;
Their cruel and winding fingers tear
Flesh from the haggard cheek and fill
The empty eye and the deaf ear.

No soft bird calls of evening reach
Beneath the muffling earth; no blue
Benignly stretching twilight sky
Can teach these eyes tranquillity.

Fixed in the postures of denial,
Those who refuted earth's sweet life
Shall have no peace in its renewal,

Only the warm rains sleeping under
Shall speak forgiveness not quite due.

E. FLORENCE SWANSON

DOUBLE SUICIDE

Now are the gates of death open unto them;
Now the long corridors invite their feet.
Death offered them a surer means of mingling
Than life could promise to their young defeat.

They would be crumbling into dust together;
They would be fortunate within the grave;
They would rise up again in the spring weather,
Stamen and pistil on a single stem.

They do not know their long disintegration
Is only bait in death's persuasive lies,—
Atom and atom as far asunder
As eyes that love are from the loved one's eyes.

E. FLORENCE SWANSON

THE LIGHT COMES BRIGHTER

The light comes brighter from the east; the caw
Of restive crows is sharper on the ear.
A walker at the river's edge may hear
A cannon crack announce an early thaw.

The sun cuts deep into the heavy drift,
Though guarded snow may still be winter-sealed.
At bridgeheads buckled ice begins to shift,
The river overflows the level field.

Once more the trees assume familiar shapes,
Their branches drop last vestiges of snow.
The water stored in narrow pools escapes
In rivulets; the cold roots stir below.

Soon field and wood will wear an April look,
The frost be gone, for green is breaking now;
The ovenbird will match the vocal brook,
The young fruit swell upon the pear-tree bough.

And soon a branch, part of a hidden scene,
The leafy mind, that long was tightly furled,
Will turn its private substance into green,
And young shoots spread upon our inner world.

THEODORE ROETHKE

HIGHWAY: MICHIGAN

Here from the field's edge we survey
The progress of the jaded. Mile
On mile of traffic from the town
Rides by, for at the end of day
The time of workers is their own.

They jockey for position on
The strip reserved for passing only.
The drivers from production lines
Hold to advantage dearly won.
They toy with death and traffic fines.

Acceleration is their need:
A mania keeps them on the move.
The edges of their nerves are frayed.
They are the prisoners of speed
Who flee in what their hands have made.

The pavement smokes when two cars meet
And steel rips through conflicting steel.
We shiver at the siren's blast.
One driver, pinned upon the seat,
Escapes from the machine at last.

THEODORE ROETHKE

THE HERON

The heron stands in water where the swamp
Has deepened to the blackness of a pool,
Or balances with one leg on a hump
Of marsh grass heaped above a muskrat hole.

He walks the shallows with an antic grace,
The great feet break the ridges of the sand,
The long eye notes the minnow's hiding place,
His beak is quicker than a human hand.

He jerks a frog across his bony lip,
Then points his heavy bill above the wood.
The wide wings flap but once to lift him up.
A single ripple starts from where he stood.

THEODORE ROETHKE

FEUD

Corruption reaps the young: you dread
The menace of ancestral eyes.
Recoiling from the serpent head
Of fate, you blubber in surprise.

Exhausted fathers thinned the blood;
You curse your legacy of pain;
Darling of an infected brood,
You feel disaster climb the vein.

There's canker at the root, your seed
Denies the blessing of the sun,
The light essential to your need.
Your hopes are murdered and undone.

The dead leap at your throat, destroy
The meaning of the day; dark forms
Have scaled your walls, and spies betray
Old secrets to primordial swarms.

You meditate upon the nerves,
Inflame with hate. This ancient feud
Is seldom won. The spirit starves
Until the dead have been subdued.

THEODORE ROETHKE

"LONG LIVE THE WEEDS"—(Hopkins)

Long live the weeds that overwhelm
My narrow vegetable realm!—
The bitter rock, the barren soil
That force the son of man to toil;
All things unholy, marked by curse,
The ugly of the universe.
The rough, the wicked, and the wild
That keep the spirit undefiled.
With these I match my little wit
And earn the right to stand or sit,
Hope, love, create, or drink and die;
These shape the creature that is I.

THEODORE ROETHKE

AUTUMNAL

The ribs of leaves lie in the dust;
The beak of frost has picked the bough;
The briar bears its thorn; and drought,
That shriveled crops before the yield,
Has left its ravage on the field.
The season's wreckage lies about,
Late autumn fruit is rotted now.
All shade is lean, the antic branch
Jerks skyward at the touch of wind,
The trees no longer hold the light,
The hedge and orchard grove are thinned.
The husk lies open to the sun:
The last of harvesting is done.
All things are brought to barn and fold,
The oak leaves strain to be unbound,
The sky turns dark, the year grows old,
The first snow sifts along the ground.

THEODORE ROETHKE

NO BIRD

Now here is peace for one who knew
The secret heart of sound;
The ear so delicate and true
Is pressed to noiseless ground.

Slow swings the breeze above her head,
The grasses whitely stir;
But in this forest of the dead
No bird awakens her.

THEODORE ROETHKE

TO MY SISTER

O my sister, remember the stars, the tears, the trains,
The woods in spring, the leaves, the scented lanes;
Recall the gradual dark, the snow's unmeasured fall,
The naked fields, the cloud's immaculate folds;
Recount each childhood pleasure: the skies of azure,
The pageantry of wings, the eye's bright treasure.

Keep faith with present joys, refuse to choose,
Defer the vice of flesh, the irrevocable choice;
Cherish the eyes, the proud incredible poise;
Walk boldly my sister but do not deign to give;
Remain secure from pain; preserve thy hate, thy heart.

THEODORE ROETHKE

INTERLUDE

The element of air was out of hand.
The rush of wind ripped off the tender leaves
And flung them in confusion on the land.
We waited for the first rain in the eaves.

The chaos grew as hour by hour the light
Decreased beneath an undivided sky.
Our pupils widened with unnatural night,
But still the road and dusty field kept dry.

The rain stayed in its cloud; full dark came near;
The wind lay motionless in the long grass.
The veins within our hands betrayed our fear.
What we had hoped for did not come to pass.

THEODORE ROETHKE

SLOW SEASON

Now light is less; noon skies are wide and deep;
The ravages of wind and rain are healed.
The haze of harvest drifts along the field,
Until clear eyes put on the look of sleep.

The garden spider weaves a silken pear
To keep inclement weather from its young.
Straight from the oak, the gossamer is hung.
At dusk our slow breath thickens on the air.

Lost hues of birds the trees take as their own.
Long since, bronze wheat was gathered into sheaves.
The walker trudges ankle-deep in leaves,
The feather of the milkweed flutters down.

The shoots of spring have mellowed with the year.
Buds, long unsealed, obscure the narrow lane.
The blood slows trance-like in the altered vein.
Our vernal wisdom moves through ripe to sere.

THEODORE ROETHKE

FLORENTINE SONG

Let the clouds dissolve
And the sun shine in upon my dreaming
Until I rise.

Holding my hands to the pure flowers
My heart to the increasing sky,
Let me hear the winds singing with birds.

O you winds,
Make a song for my heart
That I may sing it to the ever-increasing sky!

JOYCE MC INTYRE

FROM AN OPERATING TABLE

How can I die—
No marvel that the sky
Is spreading blue beyond the glass,
The silver shine
Of instruments align—
No marvel that the clouds still pass

The prevalent blue,
No marvel in the hue
Of water shimmering in a glass,
The laughing lie,
I say, how can I die?
No marvel in the untouched grass.

JOYCE MC INTYRE

SET FOR MACBETH—(*Witches' Scene*)

Mist on the cliff:
These two alone,
Stone, and the mist
Destroying the stone.

Ageless, forgotten
For time to come,
Primal water
And shapes therefrom.

Shadows lurching
Into the mist,
Merging in dream
And the sea's list,

And the low surge
Muffled and lonely—
These and the cliff:
Mist only.

FRANCES JENNINGS STILLMAN

THE CABIN—(An Old Tale)

The arrows whirred
With a soft, thin sound,
But never an arrow
Struck the ground.

And all night long
The torches glowed
Between the cabin
And the road.

The woman knew
The Indian calls
And the arrows singing
Where none falls.

They had come back
For the last to dwell
In the old log cabin
By the singing well.

Her father had gone
And his father before him,
And her son would go
Before she bore him.

She opened the door
And ran into the yard;
The cabin was drear
As an empty shard.

They found her there
In the first slow dawn
Where phantom feet
Had trampled the lawn.

And though no arrow
Was manifest,
They found a small wound
In her breast.

The townsfolk murmured
"There's naught to win
Immunity
From the wage of sin."

And the old crones babbled
Of moonbite, bedded
Within the breasts
Of the unwedded.

But when her lover
Returned to town,
He fired the cabin
And burned it down.

FRANCES JENNINGS STILLMAN

FOR LOT'S WIFE

I too have turned
   For one last look
Where the cities burned
   And the mountain shook

And know the call,
   Be it good or bad,
To run back to all
   That I ever had,

Back to the cities
   Of revel and sin
That no one pities
   As they fall in.

And I know the feeling
   Of terrible halt
When the mind stops reeling
   And turns . . . to salt!

      FRANCES JENNINGS STILLMAN

WHATEVER YOU REAP

Autumn will heap
the granaries high.
Whatever you reap,
corn, wheat or clover,
barley or rye,
when autumn is over
and winter will die,
and spring will come glazing
marsh weeds with sunlight,
whatever you reap
you will be raising
again and again.
Spring will bring rain,
the ground will be fertile,
sweet milk will curdle,
love, sour with pain;
and if you reap barley,
you will sow barley,
you will grow barley,
again and again.

ANNE PERSOV

OLD LADY

The tears came and her breath caught in her throat,
dreaming, as in a stupor, of her spent life
as child, and happy girl, and busy wife.
All she had lived and suffered seemed remote,
apart from her, as if her life had been
a story she had read that kept recurring
in memory with all the figures blurring
like dim uncertain shadows on a screen.

When she was a young girl, she recalled
how she had wished her aged great-aunt dead,
on visits through interminable hours,
when conversation lagged and silence palled.
"Be kind and take her something," her mother said,
"she can eat oranges and she likes flowers."

ANNE PERSOV

OCTOBER, RECALLED

Light frost set free the walnut. And it fell.
Fat pumpkins dozed above the blackened vine.
The frantic crows convened in fence-row trees.
There were more hazel nuts than we could find.

The tall tepees of corn were pulled apart
Where father's men had husked the hidden gold.
The long potato fields were scratched and scarred.
We had more apples than the barrels could hold.

The cellar shelves curved down beneath glass jars.
Somehow the northern autumn seemed to linger
While earth gave up the final ripened fruit.
We were not worried by the coming winter.

CHARLES MILLER

AUGUST FOR US

August simmered in the open oven of earth.
Bare spots of grass were burnt light brown.
The locust droned a nasal dirge all day.
The punctual first ripe peach came plumping down.

We found more bobolinks along the telephone wires,
And now no cheerful robins churned the silence.
We straggled down fence rows to pick wild berries
And tease the afternoon with indolence.

Beyond our woods and close to Weber's Creek
The men were mowing and raking and tumbling the marsh hay.
We brought a jug of water back to them
And bothered them a while and went away.

And wandering down the creek we suddenly caught
The Wheeler girls wading near the turn.
We captured them, wild Indians that we were,
And mastered them with all our healthy harm.

The day went slower than the lagging creek.
We dallied homeward, drawn by need of food.
The tree-hid locust zinged that metal pitch,
A fretful monotone that matched our mood.

The happy agony of August burned
In us, who did not know for what we yearned.

CHARLES MILLER

VISITATION

It was a winding road along a ridge
With moonglow for the only guiding light
Here stood a pine tree pointed like a wedge
While there below the marsh was wet and wide.

The only sounds were from the guttural frog,
From hidden crickets shrilling in response,
And beetles churning above the lumpy sod,
Or night wind fluttering through the rusty fence.

There were no meadows there: beyond the marsh
Were tangled swamps and uninviting swales;
Deformed, forbidding woods were growing sparse
And weeds were crowding clover down the hills.

Tonight I tread again that dust-white road
While clouds enmesh beneath the autumn stars,
Pausing to hear the cricket serenade,
Listening when the faint night wind recurs.

Looking at lonely land on which I grew
Where ugly hills rise barren and alone,
Where trees repulse the weak remote moonglow,
Reluctant memory will reach its home.

CHARLES MILLER

SHERIDAN COUNTY, KANSAS

From autumn docks the gangplows now embark
Upon the Kansas ocean of flat soil.
The rolling furrows fall from dawn to dark
And wash the beach away with firm recoil.
And when brown waves no longer lap this fleet
The tug-boat tractors drudge before the planter,
Dropping no anchor but the measured wheat,
Heading up the harbor of their winter.
Next autumn is a port in some far land
And so the farmer thinks of summer passed,
Seeing through falling snow the drifting sand,
Hearing in winter wind an August blast;
Remembering how he was becalmed by drouth
Until the hard brown snow blew from the south!

CHARLES MILLER

AMERICAN PASTORAL—(Deer and Oil Field)

Here, mile spaced on the cornerless, bright plain,
Where no roads intersect and roofs are lonely,
Someone has steepled black beams on the sky.
Dust settles down. The prairie wind goes slowly.

Beyond the oil wells are the funneled shacks.
A trunked cloud hangs, immense, suspended there.
No black is quite as black as carbon black.
The old buck comes; he sniffs the clouded air.

Once many deer were living in this place.
They are all gone. The buck is living still.
He is the last one of his tribe; a freak
The workingmen have not had time to kill.

A hand has pitched a stone; one leg is broken.
An antler tip was shattered, for a joke.
The old buck ranges still in these strange fields,
But strikes, now, if he sees a man approach.

He paces past the oil wells and goes on,
Savage, suspicious, frantic, and alone.
He sniffs and stares, looking again to see
Not what he knows, but all that he has known.

Here, in the map-gauged silence of the plain,
This endless country of the earth and sky,
A deer is looking for unblackened fields.
Dust rises up. The prairie wind goes by.

ELIZABETH ALLEN

HILLSCAPE—(For My Brother)

There were the slow relaxing lines of hills,
Set in the great hot blueness of the sky.
There was the dusty brush, the yellow trail,
There was an inblown sea-gull passing by.

Half hidden in the shadows of a gulch
The yucca lifted up its whitened flame.
The creek bed was a path of rippled sand.
The Indian paintbrush flowers were like their name.

A eucalyptus, full of silver wind,
Bent always, with the little weight of sound.
There was a house we had up in a tree.
There was a cave we made, a trail we found.

There was a level place where we would run
When we had climbed the last and highest hill.
I can remember just the way it was.
We could go back some day. We never will.

ELIZABETH ALLEN

MORNING SONG

The crystal jewels of morning
heap in the grass,
a young-deer wind is running
through the fruit trees,
and the maidens have come to bathe
in the river.

O their arms are wet copper branches!
Their breasts are golden apples!
Their hair shimmers blue-black
as blackbirds' wings!

They are the morning of life
the cool sweet morning!

O god of the rain!
O god of the sun!
You have made our maidens fair!

JOSEPH CHERWINSKI

SHADOWS IN THE GARDEN

My child, it is dangerous
to presume ruin and death and thunder
because your delicate veins ache.

Live in your garden,
find in your flowers messages
and rumors of new earth . . .

Aches are for sinners,
blind from the bald stare of the sun,
lame from running dark deer in private places.

Believe me, child,
in the wind and the rain
you will find treasures.

And if death come,
thunder come, and ruin,
let them come suddenly,
like clean arrows.

It is for the ancient:
the black breath, the murmur,
and the cold white jaw . . .

JOSEPH CHERWINSKI

BREATH

Your breath upon me is sweet as the breath
Of white cattle standing in blue dusk.
Like clover-honey, your breath;
Soft as the sunset murmur of white cattle,
Home from the pasture, waiting in blue dusk.

JOSEPH CHERWINSKI

PRAGUE

I think of Prague, the gargoyles dark and glum,
I feel the waltzes halted and behold
That monstrous city cold.

The ranges of the iron trees extend
Beyond the ancient distance and beyond
Still centuries of silent halls,
Bright swords inert in scabbards,
Ecclesiasts' cold cupboards,
Lean windows draping dust against the sun.

Where some philosopher of evening lifts
His mournful eyes to monuments,
There, defamed by pigeons and bereft
Of any earthly radiance,
The parchment past and its high glories blow.

And far across tall battlements, the town
Submits to darkness and the scenic night;
Cold sentinel stars are bright, and bright
The river where a suicide is found.

A child will strangle in his giant dreams,
Some housewife to the grinning soldier come,
Some poet break his knuckles on the page,
A singer crumple on an empty stage.

I think of Prague, the night's machinery done,
That fatal city in the naked dawn,
Historic and alone.

JOHN MALCOLM BRINNIN

CADILLAC SQUARE

Whoever know a city, know this square:
The loud and quaking air
That breaks on brick or scales the sun-choked glass,
The travellers who pass
One minute of one day and never more,
The neo-Grecian door
Poised like the needle's eye, open and shut
For the mythical feet
Of some squat nobleman of fields and mines,
Industrial scenes,
Or eggshell yachts afloat in summer water,
The pink expensive daughter
With a flair for shady friends and maybe Bach,
The colonnaded house and the Chinese cook.

In early spring this cobbled acre shines:
Canyoned streets, carlines
Flow with violence of union, men
Learn faith in April then;
The butcher from the suburb and the clerk
Hear the organizers speak
The resurgent language of the pioneer,
And in that press they cheer
With such a swirling and reproachless voice
The city swims in noise;
Those sooty faces and grime-sculptured hands
Live where the river bends,
They own the rotted acres made to green
Where but the fossils of machines have lain.

All interweaves among the changing years:
Progress is in arrears
Until some chanticleering message raids
The disparate multitudes,
Or the bark of some command, made sharp with hate,
Sends Property's gunmen out.
Poised in that infinity of death
Or life, or barely both,
The human balance sways; away, away,
The bleak night and the day,
The bankers couched in limousines, the poor
Jack-knifed against a door,
The bankers conscious of defeat, the poor
Jack-knifed, oblivious, against a door.

JOHN MALCOLM BRINNIN

A VISITING CARD FOR EMILY

No chronicle, melody, alarm of strings
Informed our accident of meeting here,
Nor ploughed the atmosphere
As if an almanac had so defined
This day, this town, this wind;
Up from the Cape, a lemon morning swings
With acid light for things
Fir-pointed and oblique,
Stains the Berkshires, spreads on woods to seek
Some quiet entrance to the western state
And leave us Emily for intimate.

Hail this acre for a new world's myth,
A gayer dust than all New England's quarry,
Hail this sanctuary:
Our interstellar hostess here resigned
Her transience with the blind
To life upon materials of death
Imperial monolith,
In echoing chambers made
Of gems and bones her private balustrade,
Or carved on quietude a spear, a wing;
This acre's measure is a learned thing.

Among the candelabra, high-branched, cold,
This baroque jail of her fine agony,
Silver, mahogany,
Old silence, evident of her, presides;
Its armored air recedes
To such mementoes as the mind recalled
Nor hands may ever hold;
To such remembrance as
That of Donne, of Blake, and Shelley is.
To this degree is her distinction weighed
Who took the whitest elements to wed.

This hour was life for us, who must retreat
And force our visions on the flashing east
Where now no sign is passed
That does not speak memorials to her,
Nor arrowing vistas where
She is not ultimate; quick daisies fret
No casual field, nor shut
Their buttons on a hill
But she is imminent and super-real.
How coolly now the failing sun awards
Sweet praise for Emily, her book of words.

JOHN MALCOLM BRINNIN

NEW YEAR'S EVE

Winter and aseptic snow, the last
Expected gestures of the natural year
Entrap the hemisphere;
In chambers and gaudy clubs, the cries
Of celebrants release
A rich hysteria of girls, the thin
And wine-propped arms of men,
While Sadness falls, a season of cold rain,
Since Prague is two months gone;
The shrill romantic protests have been made,
The ravaged called unfortunate, the victors mad.

That deathly epic and its legends weigh
Too mightily; the gay night is outfaced
From bleeding east to west;
A lover may not look but in his eyes
The wretched story blurs;
And yet, among the antique ruins, I trace
One luminous whole house,
A tower personal, and proudly built;
Its gay domes will not melt
Nor may the fierce designs of time unloose
Its pillars Samsonesque, its lonely peace.

Our years were young, our only crisis, love;
Desire with his scissors sharp went out
To find a grove, and cut
A tree of flowers for the double bed,
(White lilacs for your head!)
And in the slums a hundred footsteps down
The negro lights were gone,
The city skimmed on wet and summer streets
While windy curtains put
A trelliswork across your ashen eyes;
The porcelain-colored dawn flood-lit your face.

Like figures on a frieze, our partings meant
A stony history must be survived,
The disparate heart must live
Unfriended till the stone-traced pageant move;
Here was such reach of love
Would have commanded, in some other guise,
Treaties of strict peace,
Would have converted hangmen from their plans,
Deployed the raiding planes,
Put Christ in capitols and in the churches Marx,
Rung in an Easter for the orthodox.

You are not here; the frosty exit gives,
The year debased and cancerous unwinds,
Swims on through fading sounds
Into the clamped macabre pages of our text;
And whose small death is next?
Who names the untranslatable and good,
Drowned innocence in blood?
Who will evade the print, trick history,
Assume dark mastery?
The cold night moves through ether like a flame;
Loud music will not stay it, nor the lewdest name.

JOHN MALCOLM BRINNIN

ROWING IN LINCOLN PARK

You are, in 1925, my father;
Straw-hatted, prim, I am your only son:
Through zebra-light fanwise on the lagoon
Our rented boat slides on the lucent calm.

And we are wistful, having come to this
First tableau of ourselves: your eyes that look
Astonished on my nine bravado years,
My conscious heart that hears the oar-locks click

And swells with facts particular to you—
How France is Pink, how noon is shadowless,
How bad unruly angels tumbled from
That ivory eminence, and how they burned.

And you are vaguely undermined and plan
Surprise of pennies, some directed gesture,
Being proud and inarticulate, your mind
Dramatic and unpoised, surprised with love.

In silences hermetical as this
The lean ancestral hand returns, the voice
Of unfulfillment with its blade-like touch
Warning our scattered breath to be resolved.

And sons and fathers in their mutual eyes,
Exchange (a moment huge and volatile)
The glance of paralytics, or the news
Of master-builders on the trespassed earth.

Now I am twenty-two and you are dead,
And late in Lincoln Park the rowers cross
Unfavored in their odyssey; the lake
Not dazzling nor wide, but dark and commonplace.

JOHN MALCOLM BRINNIN

SANCTUS

So would I sit scarce breathing by your side
Until deflects the blunt sun from the sky,
    And the hushed winds take up, grave movemented,
To fill with night that vast and hollow eye.

    And I would sit and stare until the stars
In moving circumfixion change their place,
    And mists creep up, and quiet thoughts arise
Beyond the sharpened confines of your face.

JOHN NERBER

THE NIGHTINGALE

Was it I, who believed that within my time
The moon coexistent with my ruinous
State, and the bright contemporary nightingale
Would fail; the moon to mathematical death,
And the haunted bird from want of breath.

Who will spread my rumors, noting the exact
Date, when the great satellites crash to their fall,
When the land settles, and empty sky regains
Its cloudy impotence—O who will tell?
Not under this moon, not the nightingale will—

This was never a country of the true
Melancholy, the thickets are factories;
The voice of the motor is the voice
Of the greater; the voice of the lesser bird
Is the classic voice unheard.

The moon with the landscape of its eye
Would further the range of the nightingale's note;
Never the words in the human throat. But I
Know the shaky cries of the new world bird as frail,
Never the cries of the nightingale.

JOHN NERBER

COME PRAISE HER

Come praise her whom men desired
Beyond the thought of heaven in their youth,
Or revelry, whose wine had fired
So much their passion for her, now nearly forgot,
They fought the swarming rabble of the town;
Praise her for whom they fought
Because her name was mentioned with the name
Of one, whose memory has come down
To us, as worthy of our blame.

Was she not greater than the town
Whose men knew once and for her sake,
Better than guns, the testaments of peace;
Catullus' page held open at the knee—
The heavy mows frequented by bees
Whose golden bags were filled with sustenance
For the comely sparrow too early interred;
Or Alcuin's verse lamenting the bird
That wine might drown too deeply in his grave.

Praise her, for she is not of our time,
Though still, old men talk by the hour
Praising her beauty, drawing out in rhyme
Her deed, who lived before the last great war
In one small house from which she never stirred;
But drew her nourishment from out her store
Of borrowed books, and friends who brought them there.
O she had living from a fabulous youth;
Was fought about, had beauty for a time,
And perished, when her wit struck up the truth.

JOHN NERBER

BIOGRAPHICAL NOTES

ADAMS, MYRTLE. Mrs. Adams, born in Ontario, Canada, has lived in Detroit since 1929. She has won several prizes with her poetry and has published prose and verse in a wide variety of magazines.

ALLEN, ELIZABETH. Miss Allen was born in Syracuse, New York, "during the noise of the first World War." After graduating from the University of Michigan in 1936, she was employed for some time in the Social Service Department of the University Hospital. She is at present completing work for her master's degree at Ann Arbor. Miss Allen's poems were first published in *College Verse*. They have also appeared in *The New York Times, Fiction Parade, The Frontier and Midland,* and *The Lyric*. In 1936 she received one of the Hopwood awards in poetry at the University of Michigan.

BRINNIN, JOHN MALCOLM. Mr. Brinnin was born in Halifax, Nova Scotia, in 1916. The family moved to Detroit when he was four years old, and here he received his public school education. For several years following high school he worked in a Detroit bookstore and found time both to write poetry and to edit a literary magazine called *Prelude*. He also collaborated with John H. Thompson in editing *Signatures: Work in Progress*. His poems began to appear in various of the little magazines and shortly in such magazines as *New Masses, Life and Letters To-Day, Harper's Bazaar,* and *Poetry: A Magazine of Verse,* which in 1939 awarded him the Jeannette Sewell Davis Prize for young poets. For the last two years Mr. Brinnin has been a student at the University of Michigan, supporting himself by operating a bookstore. For the last two years he has been a recipient of a Hopwood award in poetry.

BROWN, FORMAN. Mr. Brown was born at Otsego, Michigan, in 1901 and was educated at the University of Michigan. After several years of teaching and a year of European travel he became associated with the Yale Puppeteers, principally as librettist and composer. In addition to his work with the Puppeteers (with whom he is still associated) he has found time to do a good deal of writing: radio scripts and revue material in New York; motion picture scripts in Hollywood; and two books—a collection of puppet plays, *The Pie-eyed Piper and Other Impertinent Puppet Plays* (New York: Greenberg, 1933), and a book of reminiscences, *Punch's Progress* (New York: Macmillan, 1936). *Spider Kin,* the volume from which poems in this anthology have been drawn, was published in 1929.

BURKLUND, CARL EDWIN. Mr. Burklund was born in White Cloud, Michigan, in 1897, and educated at the Western State Teachers' College, Kalamazoo, Michigan, and at the University of Michigan. He is at present a member of the Department of English, College of Engineering, of that institution. His poems have appeared in a number of magazines, including *Poetry: A Magazine of Verse, The American Poetry Journal, The English Journal, The Commonweal, Fiction Parade, The Sewanee Review,* and *The Virginia Quarterly Review*.

BUTLER, LOUISA. Miss Butler was born in Detroit in 1906. She was graduated from the University of Michigan in 1929, with honors in English. Her first poems were published at the age of fifteen in *Contemporary Verse,* then under the editorship of Charles Wharton Stork. Since that time her work has appeared in other magazines, including *The Atlantic Monthly.* She is at present a teacher in the public schools of Detroit.

CHERWINSKI, JOSEPH. Mr. Cherwinski was born in Wisconsin in 1914, but has spent most of his life in Michigan, receiving his education in the public schools of Muskegon and Lansing. He has had a varied experience as clerk, bellboy, factory hand, and free-lance writer. He has published both prose and verse: verse in *The Saturday Review of Literature, The Commonweal, The Writer,* and *The Frontier and Midland;* short stories in *New Talent* and *Tempo.*

DE JONG, DAVID CORNEL. Mr. De Jong was born in the Netherlands in 1905, but came to the United States at the age of twelve. He was graduated from Calvin College, Grand Rapids, Michigan, and studied later at Duke University. For the last five years he has been a free-lance writer. Mr. De Jong, although well known as a poet, is perhaps even better known as a novelist and short story writer. His first novel, *Belly Fulla Straw,* with Grand Rapids as its background, was published in 1934; his second, *Old Haven* (written while holding a Houghton Mifflin Literary Fellowship), was published in 1939. Over sixty of his short stories have been published, six of them reprinted in the O'Brien and the O. Henry Memorial collections. In addition he has done three translations from the Dutch: one juvenile, one biography, and one novel. Although Mr. De Jong has as yet published no volume of poetry, his work is widely printed. It has appeared in *Poetry: A Magazine of Verse, The Virginia Quarterly Review, The New Republic, The Hound and Horn,* and *The Southern Review.*

DE VRIES, CARROW. Mr. De Vries was born in Overisel, Michigan, in 1906. After graduating from high school in Holland, Michigan, he attended the University of Michigan for two years. He has been farm hand, painter, night clerk, printer, state policeman, and nightwatchman. He began writing four years ago and has published both prose and poetry in a number of newspapers and magazines.

HILL, LEONA AMES. Mrs. Hill was born in Iowa in 1904, but has lived in Michigan since 1928. Her poems have appeared in many magazines, including *The Christian Science Monitor, The Saturday Evening Post, The Ladies' Home Journal,* and *The Household Magazine.* Several of her poems have been reprinted in textbooks and anthologies for high school use.

JONES, HOWARD MUMFORD. Mr. Jones is a distinguished essayist, scholar, and critic, as well as poet. He was born in Saginaw, Michigan, in 1892, and educated at the universities of Wisconsin and Chicago. He is at present a professor at Harvard University. Among his many published works may be mentioned the following: two volumes of poems, *Gargoyles* (1918) and *They Say the Forties* (1937); *America and French Culture (1750-1848)* (1927); *The Life of Moses Coit Tyler* (1933); and *The Harp That Once* (1937), a biography of Thomas Moore. Mr. Jones is a frequent contributor to such magazines as *The Yale Review, The Atlantic Monthly, The Saturday Review of Literature, The New Republic,* and *Scribner's.* He was twice a recipient of a Guggenheim Fellowship: in 1933 and in 1936.

MILLER, CHARLES. Mr. Miller was born on a farm near Jackson, Michigan, in 1913. He attended the Jackson Junior College, Northwestern University, the Cummington School in Massachusetts (holding the Writer's Scholarship) and is at present a student at the University of Michigan. He is something of a wanderer. He has traveled, largely by the "hitchhike" method, through all of the forty-eight states and has worked in ten of them. While at Northwestern University he was one of the editors of *The Workshop,* campus literary publication. In 1939 he received one of the Hopwood awards at the University of Michigan for a group of sixty poems.

MC INTYRE, JOYCE. Miss McIntyre, born in Wisconsin in 1908, has been a resident of Michigan since the age of eleven. She is at present studying at the Western State Teachers' College, Kalamazoo, Michigan.

NERBER, JOHN. Mr. Nerber was born in Battle Creek, Michigan, "twenty odd years ago." He has been writing for three or four years and was first published in *Poetry: A Magazine of Verse.* At present Mr. Nerber is a student of John Crowe Ransom at Kenyon College, Ohio.

OLSON, IVAN. Mr. Olson, born in Sweden in 1907, came to the United States at the age of four; his family settled at Shelby, Michigan. He spent three years at Michigan State College and received his A.B. degree from the University of Michigan in 1932.

PERSOV, ANNE. Miss Persov, of Russian descent, was born in Indianapolis, in 1910, and educated at Wayne University and the University of Michigan. She has been pharmacist, teacher, artist's model, and actress. She has published short stories as well as poems; her story "Like I Was Human" received a two-star rating by O'Brien in his 1938 anthology of American stories. Her one published volume of poetry, *Whatever You Reap* (with an introduction by Max Eastman), is a collection which won a Hopwood award at the University of Michigan in 1932.

ROETHKE, THEODORE. Mr. Roethke, one of the most widely known of the younger American poets, was born in Saginaw, Michigan, in 1908. His education was received at the University of Michigan and at Harvard. He was an instructor in English at Lafayette College from 1931 to 1935, and is at present an assistant professor of English at the Pennsylvania State College. Mr. Roethke began writing in 1929, and since that time his verse and criticism have been published in most of the principal magazines of America and in many British publications. They include the following: *The Atlantic Monthly, Scribner's, The Yale Review, The New Republic, The Adelphi,* and *Poetry: A Magazine of Verse.* His poetry was featured in the November, 1934, issue of the *American Poetry Journal,* with a critical introduction by John Holmes; and a group of his poems, with critical comment by Louise Bogan, was included in the well-known anthology of younger American poets, *Trial Balances* (1935). His first volume of poems, to be called *Open House,* is scheduled for publication by Alfred A. Knopf in the spring of 1941. His most "successful" piece of writing, Mr. Roethke says, was a speech made when he was fourteen to a district Red Cross meeting. Used as propaganda, it was translated into twenty-six languages.

SMITH, A. J. M. Mr. Smith was born in Canada in 1902, attended McGill University, and later took his Ph.D. at the University of Edinburgh. Save for one short interval, he has been a member of the Department of English, Michigan State College, since 1931. Mr. Smith's work has had wide circulation and has appeared in many of the leading American and British magazines. He has contributed poetry and criticism to *The Dial, The Hound and Horn, The Nation, The Adelphi, New Verse,* and other publications. His poem "Universe Out of Stone" was included in the Moult anthology, *Best Poems of 1934,* and he was one of the Canadian poets presented in the Macmillan anthology of a few years ago, *Six Canadian Poets.*

STILLMAN, FRANCES JENNINGS. Mrs. Stillman was born in Detroit in 1910. She studied at the University of Michigan, and received an A.B. in 1931 and an A.M. in 1932. She was married to Mr. E. Clark Stillman in 1932, and from 1933 to 1939 lived abroad, mainly in Belgium and England. Her poems have been published in various magazines, including *Voices* and *Poetry: A Magazine of Verse.* In 1931 she received a Hopwood award for poetry at the University of Michigan.

SWANSON, E. FLORENCE. Miss Swanson was born in Grand Rapids, Michigan, in 1908. She was graduated from Michigan State College in 1932 and subsequently did graduate work at the University of Michigan. At present she is employed as a social worker in the Michigan Bureau of Old Age Assistance. Several of her poems have been published in *Poetry: A Magazine of Verse.*

SWIFT, IVAN. Mr. Swift was born on a farm near Dearborn, Michigan, in 1873. The family moved to the northern part of the state—the scene of so much of Mr. Swift's poetry—and here he learned printing, surveying, and telegraphy. After graduating from high school he attended the Chicago Institute of Art for three years. He was a soldier in the Spanish-American War and served in the R.O.T.C. in the World War. He makes his living as painter, craftsman, and lecturer. Mr. Swift has published two volumes of verse: *The Blue Crane and Shore Songs* and *Faggots of Cedar.* He has contributed to many magazines, including *Poetry: A Magazine of Verse, The Smart Set, The Outlook, The Independent,* and *The Forum.* His work has been reprinted in several anthologies, notably in *Songs of Horses* (Houghton Mifflin Co.) and *The Bird Lover's Anthology* (Houghton Mifflin Co.).

TEN HOOR, FREDERICK. Mr. ten Hoor was born in Franeker, the Netherlands, in 1893. He began to write, he tells us, "as an escape from Greek prepositions and Euclidean geometry." Since "escaping" high school at the end of the third year, he has been mail clerk, draftsman, soldier (with the American Expeditionary Force in France from 1917 to 1919), statistician, and controller of the V'Soske Shops, Grand Rapids, Michigan. A pithy sentence well illustrates his turn of mind: "A man alone has possibilities, but when three or more are gathered together in the name of humanity, someone is sure to be hurt." Mr. ten Hoor was first published in *The Midland,* but has appeared in a number of magazines, especially *Poetry: A Magazine of Verse.* He won the Anna Erskine award of *The Forge* in 1922 and received honorable mention in the yearly awards of *Poetry: A Magazine of Verse* for 1937.

VAN DORE, WADE. Mr. Van Dore was born in Detroit in 1899. Since leaving school at the end of the tenth grade, he has been landscape gardener, lumberman,

112

employee in the Ford factory, WPA writer, commercial artist, and hired man on New England farms. He has camped in the Canadian north woods and tramped and hoboed his way through the Canadian Rockies. Mr. Van Dore's experiences in the north woods find expression in his one published volume of poems, *Far Lake* (1930). His record includes publication in such magazines as *The New Republic, The Atlantic Monthly,* the New York *Herald-Tribune Books,* and *The London Mercury.*

WEAVER, BENNETT. Mr. Weaver was born in Wisconsin in 1892. He was educated at Carroll College, the University of Chicago, and the University of Michigan, where he has for a number of years been a member of the Department of English. In addition to various scholarly studies, Mr. Weaver has published several volumes of poems: *The Musician* (1914), *Garden of Seven Trees* (1922), and *Sussex Poems* (1926). He has contributed verse and short stories to a number of magazines.